Mid Georgian Silver

Judith Banister

COUNTRY LIFE COLLECTORS' GUIDES

The Walpole Salver. The centre shows the Exchequer Seal of George I, engraved probably by William Hogarth. Paul de Lamerie. 1728. 19¼ in square. Victoria and Albert Museum, London.

From the Rococo to the Adam Style

Numbers in the margin refer to the page where an illustration may be found

The taste for plainness of form or for simplicity allied with formal ornament that had typified silver since about 1700 could not last for ever. New men learning the craft of silversmithing had, no doubt, new ideas about design, and new patrons rejected the styles favoured by their fathers. As usual throughout the 18th century, even when England was at war with her, France provided the main inspiration for change. The 'Régence' style of the years immediately following Louis XIV's death in 1715 soon flowered into the Rococo, with its eternal movement, its marine fantasies, its waves and scrolls. All the ingredients of the Rococo were, of course, still basically Renaissance motifs, though they were no longer formal and regular, but asymmetrical and flowing.

The style came slowly to England and it was not until after the accession of George II in 1727 that the Rococo began to influence English silver. During the 1730s, flat-chasing, with its soft outline patterns, began to give way to richer and more pronounced ornament. Detail became three-dimensional, with much use of casting and of chasing executed in high relief. Bold swirls, shells and scrolls, grotesque masks and rocky surfaces were a romantic rebellion against formality.

Some of the most spectacular silver ever made in England was produced during the middle years of the 18th century, by men such as Paul de Lamerie, Paul Crespin, his neighbour Nicholas Sprimont (soon to become manager of the new Chelsea porcelain factory), Thomas Farrer, Charles Kandler and many others. With tremendous confidence, they created designs that, viewed analytically, seem to have little kin with the wares themselves: sea serpents formed the spouts of tea-kettles, cherubs peered out among the foliage on baskets, caryatids turned and twisted among the rocks, seaweed, shells and scrolls of everything from candlesticks to soup tureens.

For the most part, they were successful, though even the greatest craftsmen sometimes made functional mistakes. Superbly worked jugs and kettles by Lamerie, for instance, could be awkward to hold and harder to clean, while Charles Kandler's wonderfully made **sauce boats**, such as those in the Ashmolean Museum, Oxford, are not very practical if one considers that they were intended for hot sauce, and to feel comfortable holding them one really needs gardening gloves. What they lacked in functional quality, however, they made up for in virtuosity—a natural feeling for line and ornament never achieved in the efforts of, for instance, the Regency craftsmen, who even at their best betrayed a self-consciousness about design.

The magnificent silver-gilt ewer and dish by Paul de Lamerie made in 1741 for the Goldsmiths' Company, whose arms are chased in the centre of the dish in high relief. The rim is also richly chased. Width 31 in. The ewer (height $14\frac{3}{4}$ in.) has the handle formed as a marine god. The Worshipful Company of Goldsmiths, London.

Lesser silversmiths of the mid 18th century did not, on the whole, attempt the wilder flights of the Rococo, but adapted its themes to their own capabilities and to the tighter purses of their patrons. As a rule the standard of silversmithing was high, the gauge of metal used was fairly heavy, except in some smaller wares towards the end of the period, and most silversmiths were well able to handle applied and cast ornament, and employed skilled chasers and engravers in their busy workshops. Demand for silver remained prodigious at all levels, despite the tax at the rate of 6d. an ounce, which had been imposed in 1720 when the sterling standard was restored.

The wealthiest patrons ordered vast quantities of silver in the latest fashion, others added to family collections, sometimes choosing the exuberant and lavish Rococo styles, sometimes preferring decorative versions of existing silver, so that many pieces were still made in what was really the Baroque style, applied shells, scrolls and perhaps an asymmetrical finial being almost the only real concessions to the new ornament. But, high

The sauceboat gave great scope for Rococo ornament, as in this much chased version with eagle handle and the sides chased with birds, fish and animals amid Rococo scrolls, shells and other motifs. Charles Kandler. 1742. Conway Gift, Ashmolean Museum, Oxford.

fashion or not, this was the great age of silver in England, with a vast output of all kinds of wares: for the dining-room and the drawing-room, for the punch drinker and the tea drinker, silver for lighting and the toilet, for actual use or simply for decoration.

The trouble with such a distinctive and even overpowering style as the Rococo was not only function. There is a limit to the variations on the fantasies; the very exuberance of the style began to cloy. In time, when the shells and C-scrolls, asymmetrical sprays of flowers and foliage were to be seen everywhere, the leaders of taste began to seek new ideas. About 1745 there was a revival, for the second time in less than a century, of oriental motifs. This time, instead of the naive engraved and flat-chased scenes used in the 17th century, there was a more sophisticated approach, influenced largely by Chinese export porcelain. Eastern themes were used for all kinds of cast and chased work, but most especially on tea-table wares. Like the Chinese artists of the period, the designers were quite prepared to mix Chinese and European motifs, so that long-robed mandarins and elegant English ladies languishing under parasols, oriental temples and native straw huts, orange trees and palm trees, English flowers and tea-plants appear charmingly intermixed with Rococo shells and scrolls.

By the late 1750s, for those tired of the Rococo and not attracted by the 'gaudy gout of the Chinese', there was as yet no newly emergent style. A few of the London silversmiths began once more to look to France for inspiration, but the gilded splendour of Louis XV's court was not to the English taste – though some of its more restrained themes, such as the reed-and-tie border and the shallow bombé form were used with some success by one or two of the leading London silversmiths, such as Parker & Wakelin or Courtauld & Cowles. A few even tried out 'Gothick' designs. Between about 1760 and 1770, however, most made a sort of negative return to the Baroque, which had never quite been banished, and an inclination towards its classical inspiration was, in the last years of the decade, to sweep in with all the ordered splendour and direct classicism that we call the Adam style.

Silver for Lighting, Writing and Display

Whereas today lighting equipment is part of the furniture, in 18th-century England there were few lighting fixtures, except for the sconce and the chandelier, and the silver candlestick was a necessary piece of furnishing. The period of around 1760 saw the development of the loaded, instead of the cast, candlestick, due largely to factory production of stamped parts in Sheffield.

The cast baluster candlestick, with a **tapering vase-shaped stem**, was well established at the beginning of the period, fluted angles at the corners of the square base often being repeated in miniature on the shoulders. Gradually, without changing the basic form, more and more decoration appeared: the base was given incurved sides and chased with **masks and scrolls** at the corners, and knops, shoulders and sconce were applied with shells, foliage and husks.

Some silversmiths specialised in different aspects of the craft, and the Cafe and Gould families were especially noted for candlesticks. Most of the their work was relatively formal, the really exotic designs being the work of leading designer-craftsmen such as Paul de Lamerie, John Jacobs, and James Shruder.

The highly decorative cast Rococo candlestick was a masterpiece of movement and chasing in relief. Shells, scrolls, foliage, flowers and masks overlaid the basic baluster form, and this was sometimes swirled, in the manner of the French designer Meissonier, so that the asymmetry of the Rococo themes was brought out in cartouche-like sides on the stem. Bases became rocky

left Typical baluster candlestick on shaped square base with fluting on angles and on shoulders. Made in London in 1742, probably by George Wickes. Height 8¼ in. Private collection.

below left One of a pair of candlesticks of 1741 by the Huguenot Edward Feline, showing French influence. Applied with winged masks on the scalework sides of the bases, medallion heads on the chased stems. Private collection.

below Rococo asymmetry of scrolls and flowers on a candlestick from a set of four by Paul de Lamerie. 1749. Private collection.

promontories, chased shells and scrolls rose up the stems to shell-encrusted nozzles. For the patrons who wanted decorative magnificence, there were innumerable, though rare, variations: kneeling negroes holding up an acanthus-girt stem, scrolling bases supporting twisted columns, shaped triangular bases rising

9 to **demi-figures eternally holding flower-chased sockets**.

Throughout the 1750s Rococo themes dominated, hinted at in the less costly examples, elaborately treated in the grander candlesticks. However, some attempts were made towards simplicity, and about 1755 the first Corinthian column types

11 appeared, and **gadrooned square bases** with tall many-knopped and fluted stems typified candlesticks of the 1760s. By then height was all-important, most being about ten inches high or

Pair of figure candlesticks with shaped richly chased bases, by Paul de Lamerie. 1748. One shows a male, the other a female, caryatid supporting the scrolling sconce. Conway Gift, Ashmolean Museum, Oxford.

even more. A few silversmiths made excursions into new realms—a rare set made in 1765 by Frederick Kandler shows **Gothic**

11   **cluster columns** chased with quatrefoils; another set of 1767–1771 by William Cripps is formally chased with reed-and-tie borders in the French manner, and in 1770 Thomas Heming created a series of figure candlesticks with draped female stems and foliate cornucopiae forming the sconces. However, as early as 1768 John Carter had made the first candlesticks to Adam's design, and within ten years, the new classicism was firmly established.

11   Branched candlesticks, or **candelabra**, were much in keeping with Georgian love of display. The earliest complete candelabrum, appearing to date from 1731, was a suite made by George Wickes for the Prince of Wales, but many candelabra are in fact standard candlesticks, provided, often some years later, with two, three or four branches.

A much needed light in the Georgian home was the chamber candlestick, a large-panned hand candlestick which the guests would take to their rooms. Most of these were simple, shaped shell and scroll borders and leaf-capped thumb-pieces for the scroll handle often being their only ornamental features.

Naturally snuffers to trim the wicks of the candles were needed.

11, 12   By 1730, the usual stand was a **snuffer tray**, the hour-glass shape with a back handle being far the most popular. The making of the snuffers appears to have been another specialist job, so that matching stands and snuffers are exceedingly rare.

Besides candles for light, tapers were used for softening wax

12   for sealing letters and so on. **Tapersticks** were generally miniature versions of the cast candlestick, either made in pairs to be set on each side of the table or desk, or singly, to be the centrepiece of an inkstand. About 1745 the charming harlequin pattern was introduced—a figure in motley dress and wide hat holding above his head the fluted waxpan and sconce. Occasionally during the 1760s other figures were used—one taperstick of 1761 has a sailor, another, of 1765, had a girl holding a flower.

13, 14   **Inkstands**, or standishes as they were called, were dishes or trays fitted with ink and pounce pots, a well for pens and some-

left Gadrooned square base on a formal cast candlestick. William Cafe. 1763. Height $10\frac{1}{4}$ in. The Cafe family were noted makers of candlesticks. Private collection.

right Candelabra became fashionable during the period; this set of 1750 comprises four candlesticks by Paul de Lamerie with two two-light branches, probably by the same maker but unmarked. Formerly in the collection of Earl Howe.

below Rare 'Gothic' candlestick from a set of four. Frederick Kandler. 1765. Height $14\frac{1}{4}$ in. They are loaded, as were many candlesticks from about 1760 onwards.

below An unusual snuffers tray with flat-chased ornament and chased border of flowerheads. Paul de Lamerie. 1734. Private collection.

above Typical hourglass-shaped snuffers tray with leaf-capped back handle, four hoof feet and shell motifs at corners. William Hunter. 1748. Private collection.

left Taperstick with gadrooned borders. Ebenezer Coker. 1763. Height $6\frac{1}{2}$ in. Private collection.

times a taperstick, a small pot for wafers or a bell. The usual form of stand was oblong with an everted moulded rim and baluster pots. Then came the shaped oval, and by 1740 Lamerie and other leading designers were making very elaborate styles.

14 One of the most lavish is **that made by Lamerie** for the Goldsmiths' Company in 1741, incorporating the bell given to the Company by Sir Robert Vyner in 1666. The oblong stand is gilt and decorated with asymmetrical scrolls and garlands of flowers, and at each corner there is a different classical mask in high relief. Almost as outstanding is an inkstand of 1744 by John Edwards, with a scrolling base in the style of Meissonier and a Rococo cartouche flanked by eagles' wings in the centre. At either end are dolphin masks and shells, while there are more

Inkstand or standish with baluster-shaped ink and pounce pots, bell and well for pens. William Cripps. 1749. Private collection.

dolphins on a most unusual pair of bowls in the centre. Vying with these masterpieces is Paul Crespin's shell-shaped standish of 1739, now at Chatsworth, a confection of shells and coral in silver-gilt.

Most writers were, however, content with simple trays, oblong or oval, and often quite plain even at the height of the Rococo period. The corrosive properties of 18th-century ink made silver-mounted glass pots a sensible proposition, and from about 1755 there was a trend towards having these mounted in pierced galleried frames – work often done by firms such as Herbert & Co. and William Plummer, who specialised in pierced work.

The table bell, either alone or as part of the inkstand, was inevitably a simple design, usually with a central rib and a baluster handle. At any period, bells are rare.

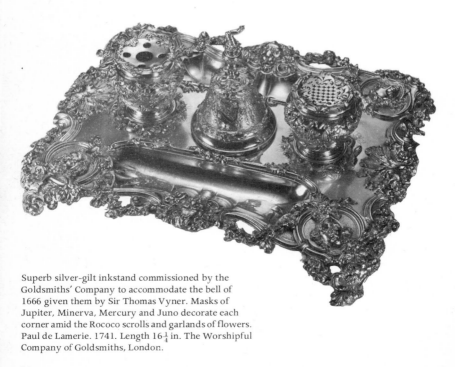

Superb silver-gilt inkstand commissioned by the Goldsmiths' Company to accommodate the bell of 1666 given them by Sir Thomas Vyner. Masks of Jupiter, Minerva, Mercury and Juno decorate each corner amid the Rococo scrolls and garlands of flowers. Paul de Lamerie. 1741. Length 16¼ in. The Worshipful Company of Goldsmiths, London.

Much in evidence was the salver or waiter, made in all sizes from about six inches to as much as twenty or twenty-two inches across. In the small sizes, today usually called waiters (although in fact in the past silversmiths applied the term to all sizes) sets of four were sometimes made, and pairs were common, sometimes accompanied by a larger matching waiter. Most were circular, but oblongs and squares with cut corners were much favoured. On the more expensive waiters, flat-chased strapwork borders below the moulded rim and elaborate cartouches containing the owner's armorials gradually became more and more elaborate, while there was a great variety of different borders – the **Bath**, with its plain flowing outline, the more accentuated '**Chippendale**', and plainer moulded versions with guilloche or other decorative edge mounts. The shaped border, embellished at

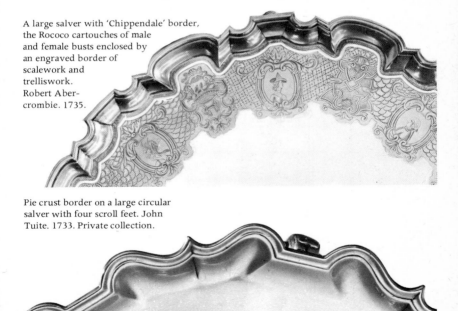

A large salver with 'Chippendale' border, the Rococo cartouches of male and female busts enclosed by an engraved border of scalework and trelliswork. Robert Abercrombie. 1735.

Pie crust border on a large circular salver with four scroll feet. John Tuite. 1733. Private collection.

right Salver with flat-chased
shells and scrolls below a shaped
moulded border chased with
sprays of foliage at intervals.
John Jacobs. 1737. Width 12¾ in.
Private collection.

below Large salver with cast,
chased and pierced border of
vines, masks and shells. Paul de
Lamerie. 1739. Diameter 19 in.
Formerly in the Ionides
collection.

16   intervals with **shells, scrolls and other motifs**, remained popu-
     lar throughout the period. From about 1740 a number of fine
     salvers were made with intricate **cast, chased and pierced**
16   **mounts**. Vines, shells, masks and intertwined foliage and flowers
     created wonderful patterns of light and shade, varied in the later
     1750s by chinoiserie motifs—Chinese heads, pagoda-like designs
     and 'Chinese Chippendale' fretwork patterns. Some of these larger
     and more important salvers were probably in fact tea-trays, or
     tea-tables, as they were called.

     The making of trays and salvers is a very skilled and specialised
     craft of the silversmith, and the middle years of the century saw
     a number of notable salver makers, including John Tuite, Robert
     Abercromby and George Hindmarsh, many of whose pieces were
     of a standard often only associated with the 'great' makers.

     The great makers were, of course, employed on making fine
     silver and silver-gilt masterpieces to be used and displayed in the
     grand saloons, the imposing dining-rooms, and the long galleries
     in stately houses up and down the country. Some such work was
     frankly ornamental, such as the **massive silver-gilt ewer and**
4   **basin** of 1741 made by Lamerie for the Goldsmiths' Company.
     The broad rim of the dish is repoussé chased with classical figures
     among Rococo ornament, while the centre of the dish is taken up
     with the arms of the Company in high relief. The ewer, one of the
     rare examples of ewers made during the period, is helmet-shaped
     in the traditional manner, and exhibits all the virtuosity of rich-
     ness and chasing that Lamerie could muster.

     Akin to such rare display plate were the commemorative
     salvers made from the exchequer seals—the finest and most
     famous of all being that made in 1728 for Sir Robert Walpole,
2   Chancellor at the time of George I's death in 1727. The **salver**, sold
     in 1956, went to the Victoria and Albert Museum. Again, the
     maker was Paul de Lamerie, and the piece is exquisitely engraved,
     almost certainly by Hogarth, with a central medallion showing
     both faces of the seal held up by Hercules and other allegorical
     figures against a background panorama of London.

18, 19, 20   The **cup and cover** remained, however, the most usual form
     for purely ornamental silver, and it is evident that many were

Shells, scales and fishy shapes
dominate this silver-gilt cup. Paul de
Lamerie. 1737. Height 15 in. The
Fishmongers' Company, London.

Silver-gilt cup and cover by Thomas Farren, one of four made for the Goldsmiths' Company in 1740. One scroll handle terminates in a satyr's head, the other in that of a bacchante. The arms of the Company appear on one side, while the other shows a figure of Minerva in high relief. Height 15¼ in. The Worshipful Company of Goldsmiths, London.

considered as expositions of the latest styles and finest silversmithing available. The bell-shape with applied strapwork round the body and two bold scroll handles remained the basic form, but during the 1730s the strapwork became more elaborate, often against a matted ground for greater contrast. Rococo ebullience and asymmetry in fact came early to the design of cups and covers –one cup by Lamerie, dated 1732, has four figures symbolising the seasons between festoons of foliage and fruit instead of the usual applied straps. The scroll handles are richly chased with amorini and vines, scrolls, foliage, shells and scalework, and even hounds' heads are arranged in orderly disorder around the foot, while dragon, dolphin, eagle and lion masks, musical trophies and serpents, shells and vines adorn the domed cover.

With the next few years, formal upright straps inevitably became **swirling scrolling patterns**, interspersed with masks and shells; finials became bunches of grapes or even vegetables

19

or fruit, or they rose to high pinnacles. Many cups were large, over a foot high, and weighing as much as 100 ounces or more. Often the terminals of each handle would be different—a satyr on one, or perhaps a bacchante on the other, as in the cups and covers made in 1740 by Thomas Farren for the Goldsmiths.

20 By about 1750, the **shaped body with a bulging lower section** ousted the bell-shape. **Vines** and snakes were favourite motifs, overlaying bodies and handles and covers in high relief. Everything was rich and beautifully executed—whether it was a tiny model of a lizard or the figure of Pan, chasing in high relief or wave-like fluting. It was this ability to create large and splendid pieces of display plate that was to prove an invaluable asset to the silversmith when, during the 1770s, Adam and his designers demanded all the skills of modeller and chaser to create silver in the manner of carved marble.

The Esso Cup, a silver-gilt cup and cover, richly chased with vines, insects and snails over the fluted vase-shaped body, has a domed cover topped by an infant Bacchus and handles formed as Pan and a nymph. Thomas Heming. 1759. Height $16\frac{1}{2}$ in. Bequeathed by The Esso Petroleum Co. Victoria and Albert Museum, London.

Silver for the Dinner Service

One of the most notable developments affecting silver during the first half of the 18th century was the increased variety of wares made for the dining-table: soup tureens, sauce boats, épergnes, mazarins, mustard-pots, cruets and **dish-crosses** were introduced to supplement the already established dishes and plates, casters, salts, bread and cake baskets, dessert and sweetmeat dishes and bowls and, of course, flatware and cutlery. However, the matching dinner service as we understand it was a much later innovation, and though occasionally some effort was made to have tureens and sauce boats, for example, or dishes and plates en suite, most dining-table silver was assembled, and relied for its unity simply on the style of the period in which it was made.

The soup tureen was perhaps the most important of dining-table silver. The 18th-century idea of soup was much more substantial than most soups of today, rather in the nature of minestrone, meat stew and bouillabaisse, and wealthy householders gave due prominence to the soup tureen. It was generally a large, heavy and costly piece of plate, and on it was lavished all the craftsmanship associated with the latest fashionable styles. Most tureens were capacious, holding up to about six quarts; they were usually oval, though sometimes circular, and with a cover. A high foot or four cast feet steadied the tureen and kept it from contact with the table top, and end-handles usually made carrying easier, though some tureens were also provided with a large dish or sometimes a stand.

41

The tureen, perhaps more than any other piece of domestic silver, allowed the silversmith scope for his individuality. In 1728 and 1729, Charles Kandler made **a series of tureens**, some with stands, fluted in the style of German Rococo, their scroll handles and finials almost the only concession to ornament. It is significant that these Kandler tureens, as well as all Lamerie's work before 1732, were of the higher Britannia standard (see page 61), though it was no longer obligatory.

During the next decade, all the ingredients of the Rococo, with much chasing in high relief, applied work, cast detail and modelling, were used with considerable ingenuity on tureens, and the interchange of designs and themes among the London silversmiths is a subject of great fascination. In 1733 Paul Crespin made

Formal fluted soup tureen, cover and stand with voluted scroll handles. In the higher Britannia standard. Charles Kandler. 1728. Private collection.

a tureen decorated with plain straps and foliate ones on a matted ground between the four really ferocious lion-mask knuckles. It was paired with another of 1738 by George Wickes, and was the property of Sir Robert Walpole. A third tureen of identical design was made about the same time by Benjamin Godfrey. A grandly Rococo tureen of 1739 by John Edwards, with a pair bearing the maker's mark only, had unusual boar's head handles –a device that Edwards repeated on an otherwise much more elaborate Rococo tureen of 1746, and which Lamerie also chose to use in the same year.

In 1737 John Edwards created a tureen which really seemed to mix **all the Rococo themes**–large shell and scroll feet, an oval body hung with applied flower festoons around a Rococo car-

23

Dolphin handles and a crab finial dominate this superb and rare tureen of 1737 by John Edwards, a master of the Rococo style. Width $16\frac{1}{4}$ in. Private collection.

touche on either side, dolphin handles, and shells and rockwork surrounding a scalework ground from which rises a model of a crab – very much in the manner of contemporary porcelain. Even more exotic are the Paul Crespin tureens of 1740 and 1741. The first, now in Toledo Museum of Art, Ohio, is an oval hidden between flower festoons and resting on the backs of two models of hinds; between them rests an orange and a lemon, while the cover is heavy with modelled life-size fruit – grapes, plums, apples and pears. The whole rests on a large stand $21\frac{3}{4}$ inches long, and weighs 524 ounces. The later tureen, in the royal collection, is a yet more elaborate **centrepiece with a marine theme**, the elegant oval tureen supported by mermaids and dolphins with the whole topped with a figure of Neptune.

24

Marine themes carried out in superb modelling and chasing on a silver-gilt tureen centrepiece by Paul Crespin, 1741. Height 27 in. Royal Collection.

The double-lipped sauceboat survived into the mid Georgian period, usually with a little decorative detail, such as the shells chased below the lips of this pair of 1730 by Pezé Pilleau. Private collection.

Many tureens were, however, relatively plain, with lion-mask knuckles and claw-and-ball feet, leaf-decorated scroll handles and occasionally flower sprays chased or applied on the sides of otherwise fairly plain bombé oval shapes. A modelled bird, vegetable or other finial might be the only truly Rococo aspect. By 1750, taste for lavish tureens seems entirely to have abated. Shapes became a little shallower, with a shaped rim, the wavy outline echoed in a gadroon or guilloche mount on the cover. A rare style had overall stepped and fluted decoration, rising to a pagoda-like finial, or, in a more condensed form, decorated with a pattern rather like quilting. Such styles marked time before the Neo-classical period and, indeed, continued in favour long after the impact of Adam.

Judging from the number and variety of sauce boats in England, Voltaire must have visited some rather ungastronomic houses to suggest there was only one English sauce. The accession of George II actually coincided with a new shape for the sauce boat—with single lip and a handle opposite instead of a **double-lipped boat-shape with side handles**. Two versions appeared in 1727—a plain oval on a stepped moulded foot, and a style with mounted rim and four hoof feet. At first the former style was more usual, but about 1735 the type on four cast feet came into general use. On the whole, however, the practical overruled the decorative. Decoration was chiefly restricted to lion-mask, shell or foliate knuckles, and occasionally applied Rococo festoons.

25

Much 18th-century porcelain imitated silver originals. Here it seems that early Chelsea inspired these vine-leaf pattern sauceboats by Philip Brugier, made in 1755. The bodies are formed as leaves on which are chased a butterfly, a bee and a beetle. Private collection.

By 1740, however, a few of the leading silversmiths were creating styles very akin to those soon to be made in porcelain: nautilus-shell boats with sea-serpent handles and feet, and Rococo extravaganzas such as those by Charles Kandler, of which there are three different pairs in the Ashmolean Museum at Oxford. But while only a few essayed pieces on rocky bases, overlaid with all sorts of tiny models of insects and animals, many used shell motifs for feet, and made rims scalloped or gadrooned and interspersed with shells and foliage. Exotic flying-scroll handles also suggested the Rococo—dolphins, serpents and eagles' heads were an ornamental variation of the usual scroll and foliate patterns. Makers using shell-shaped bodies tended to stabilise the base with a central foot, usually oval, enriched with fluting or chased with shells, foliage and so on, or even by inverted intertwined dolphins. The Rococo themes of the potters seem to have been interpreted in silver by a pair of sauce or cream boats actually formed as leaves to which are applied butterflies, beetles and bees—even the loop handles are formed as twigs.

About 1765 two innovations appeared at the dinner-table. One was the sauce tureen, a smaller version of the soup tureen, usually with end handles and cover to keep the sauce hot on the long journey from the kitchen quarters. The other was the argyll, or argyle, a vessel for keeping gravy hot, the heat retained by a hot-water jacket or a heated iron. Most argyles were plain cylindrical vessels, with straight or curved spouts, the handle usually opposite, though occasionally at right-angles to the spout. The earliest recorded argyle dates from 1755, but they were very rare until 1765.

The baluster caster, first introduced at the beginning of the century, is surely one of the most satisfying of all silver designs. The sturdy foot, circular or octagonal according to the outline of the body, balances perfectly the high domed cover with its
27 **intricate piercing** – itself a subject for wonder when it is realised that until about 1760 piercing was done with hammer and chisel, not with a saw. Even during the Rococo era, few casters were much ornamented, except so far as the piercing was concerned, though a few outstanding examples were lavished with **applied**
29 **festoons** or chased detail by the leading silversmiths. Again, however, caster making tended to be done by specialist makers, the chief castermaker of the mid Georgian period being Samuel Wood, whose output was prodigious.

About 1755, however, even the simple baluster caster was
28 given a Rococo interest, when **spiral fluting** came in fashion, a

right Sugar caster with Rococo pierced cover. Paul de Lamerie. 1732. Height 8$\frac{1}{4}$ in. Private collection.

below By the end of the period, the sauce tureen gradually superseded the sauceboat. These open tureens and stands by the royal goldsmith, Thomas Heming, 1761, were part of Speaker's plate issued to Sir John Cust, and formed part of the Brownlow collection.

theme followed out even to the twisted-flame finial. It was no great transition from that to the taller vase-shape, used for all sizes, from tall sugar casters to tiny versions for pepper and spices. Sets of casters, still usually made in trios, were often provided with a ring frame to form a cruet, partnered sometimes by another cruet for oil and vinegar bottles, or combined, as in the Warwick cruets. The frames for oil and vinegar bottles were often rather more ornamental than those for casters only, for the glass bottles with their silver handles and neck mounts were slender and needed support in a deep frame, sometimes pierced in intricate Rococo designs, but often still relatively plain, even at the height of the Rococo period.

Mustard pots in the familiar drum-shape were a product of the 1760s. Before that, dry mustard was usually served in one of the small casters of a set, the top being left 'blind' or unpierced. Mixed mustard was perhaps served in a shallow dish, or saucer. The first mustard pots in their own right were barrel-shaped, and date back to 1724. There is also one with a **harp-shaped handle**, made in 1747 by Edward Wakelin, in the Ashmolean, but it

29

Samuel Wood was a prolific maker of casters and cruets. Here three spirally fluted casters are included in a cruet stand on shell feet with a Rococo cartouche at the front for the owner's arms. Made in 1756. Private collection.

right Very early mustard pot with applied strapwork on a matted ground round the base of the bell-shaped body. Edward Wakelin. 1747. Ashmolean Museum, Oxford.

below Set of three baluster casters, made by Paul de Lamerie in 1738 but with the mark overstruck by another, possibly Phillips Garden. Cast chased detail and intricate asymmetrical piercing exemplify the high Rococo style. Private collection.

was the age of fine piercing, the 1760s, that brought the mustard pot with its pretty blue glass liner showing through a fret of scrolls, flowerheads and foliage. The cover was in most cases flat, and there was a pierced or shell-shaped thumbpiece and a simple scroll handle.

The small salts known as trencher salts began early in the period to change from the standard octagonal form to the small pedestal bowl, which was a better vehicle for applied or chased ornament; stiff foliage round the base and a formal border round the foot were not uncommon. On the round-bellied type, standing on three or four feet, even more decoration could be applied, and other Rococo themes used. From about 1730 onwards, most salts were of this type—variations included lion-mask and paw feet, shell knuckles, hoof feet, and, in the special salts of the most expensive silversmiths, even sea serpents and other fantasies. Many salts were, however, the work of specialist makers, such as the Woods and the firm of Hennell, which was founded by David Hennell in 1736.

30   The 1750s saw a revival of the **pedestal salt**, interspersed with some charming and rare Rococo designs such as naturalistic shells

Circular pedestal salt with applied leafage and foliage-chased foot. Simon Le Sage. 1758. Private collection.

right Chinoiserie pierced salts on shell feet have everted rims which unscrew to hold the cagework bodies round the glass liners. By Emick Romer, a Norwegian silversmith working in London. About 1760. Private collection.

below Butter dishes with naturalistic encrusted shell feet. Parker & Wakelin. 1766. Private collection.

and one or two rather grotesque designs incorporating sea monsters, wave-like grounds and rocky bases. Even the tea-table chinoiserie fashion made its occasional appearance on salts, with 31 **pierced designs** fitted with glass liners.

The shell theme, so appropriate to the Rococo, was used for dishes themselves, and some of the finest examples of scallop-
31 shaped dishes appear to have been cast from actual **scallop shells**. One record of 1740 mentions an account for '5 Scollops for Oysters', for which indeed they may have been used, but they were equally suitable for butter (they are usually called butter-shells nowadays), preserves, pickles and the like. They were usually made in pairs or larger sets, and the conceit of using whelk or snail shapes for the feet, probably introduced by David Willaume, continued throughout the period.

Taste for plainness or taste for decoration were both equally well catered for by the makers of silver baskets. The period began with formally pierced oval baskets and ended in a fantasy of chinoiseries. Most mid Georgian baskets were circular or oval, **silver replicas of wickerwork baskets**, the sides interwoven even to the hooped border, and with ropework handles at either side under the flared rim. The centres, usually unpierced, were elegantly engraved with coats of arms in Baroque cartouches. Even the early 1730s lacked highly decorated baskets, and they relied for their attraction on the play of light through the latticed sides. Fixed or swing handles were, however, introduced about 1730 as an alternative to end-handles, and gradually the moulded rim foot was ornamented with more elaborate piercing. By 1735 one of the leading masters of ornamental table baskets, Peter Archambo, of Huguenot descent, was moving away from 'wicker-work' sides to those **pierced out in scrolls and arabesques**, with applied Rococo shell details along the sides. By now, most baskets were oval, and within a year or two a few of the most lavish baskets were being supplied with cast 'apron' supports, their everted rims mounted with Rococo shell and scrollwork, and the formerly plain bases became vehicles for fine **diaper** and other flat-chased ornament which was placed around the armorials of the owner.

During the 1740s the baskets tended to become shallower, many more were mounted on heavily cast and chased feet, and the border mounts were enriched with vines and scrolls, cherubs' heads and shells above the pierced panels of diaperwork that covered the spreading sides. Even the swing handles were elaborate, applied with shells, terminating in scrolls and even in caryatid figures, and engraved or chased with bands of flowers and foliage. Throughout the 1740s it seems as though the major silversmiths – Paul de Lamerie, David Willaume, Peter Archambo, Augustine Courtauld, the Godfreys and many others – were vying with one another to produce the most elegant and magnificent baskets for the bread, cakes and fruit at table.

About 1750 there was a change of taste, a reversion to the less extravagant designs of the 1730s. Rim mounts in particular were lighter both in weight and in style, narrower shell and scroll

Wickerwork inspired silver cake basket with twisted ropework handle. Paul de Lamerie. 1734. Formerly in the collection of Lord Rothermere.

Intricate Rococo scroll, shell and foliage border and apron foot for an oval cake basket, the base chased with rocaille designs and the sides pierced with scrolls and diaperwork. John Jacobs. 1737. Private collection.

motifs, or wheatear and mask designs giving point to, rather than overshadowing, the piercing of the sides. Cast feet—scrolls, shells, and even dolphins—were frequently enriched with cast, chased and pierced aprons of flowers with other Rococo motifs between, but there was often more emphasis on **openwork designs**, with the piercing extending right to the applied rim. Some of the leading basketmakers such as Herbert & Co. and Aldridge & Stamper even reproduced the wickerwork style in graceful everted baskets, piercing out the handles in ovals and returning to an oval rim foot pierced in vertical cuts.

During the 1760s there was a fashion for baskets with panels of different piercings between snaking beaded outlines—often three or four different styles of piercing would be used in a single basket. Wirework was also popular, and some baskets were quite plain, the vertical bands held between a gadrooned rim and a plain base, or, in one of the most charming baskets of the late 1760s, intertwined with foliage, flowers, wheatears and bunches of grapes—a late essay in the Rococo.

Parallel with and complementary to basket design between 1730 and 1770 was the **silver épergne, or centrepiece**, composed of series of dishes and small baskets on a central stand. Surviving épergnes before the mid 1750s are very rare, and the first ones appear to have been designed for dessert dishes, or to accommodate various table silver such as casters, candlesticks and cruets. One such is a large épergne by David Willaume and Ann Tanqueray, dated 1731, with a central bowl, two sets of casters, two pairs of oil and vinegar bottles, four candle-holders, and, to replace bowl and candlesticks, four circular, and one large, oval dessert dishes, with all the strapwork, chased and pierced work executed in great detail.

During the 1750s, the épergne continued chiefly as a central dessert bowl or basket surrounded by smaller dishes and sometimes incorporating candleholders. In 1753 Thomas Heming made a Rococo épergne surmounted by a canopy—a style that was to reach its peak in the **chinoiserie épergnes** of the early 1760s, where the Chinese taste was charmingly interpreted with bell-hung canopies, figures of mandarins and coolies and Chinese

35

35, 36

36

Panels of different patterns of piercing divided by beading on a cake basket in late style. Herbert & Company. 1763. Private collection.

The Newdigate Centrepiece, one of the earliest épergnes in English silver, shows Rococo treatment of dishes and stand. Paul de Lamerie. 1743. Width 20 in. Victoria and Albert Museum, London.

masks accompanying the Rococo flowers and foliage and scroll-work of the pierced frames. By 1760, Thomas Pitts was established as one of the leading makers in London, and his variations on the theme of épergnes were legion. Sometimes baskets were set in circular or oval frames, sometimes they hung from the branches; candleholders might rise among the branches, or silver dishes and baskets be replaced by light-looking glass-mounted bowls. One of Pitt's variations from about 1766 onwards was a centrepiece with unpierced petal-like bowls and candle-sconces set among the curving branches, but generally speaking he and other makers, such as Vere & Lutwyche and Emmick Romer, produced basket-épergnes as tall centrepieces to grace the centre of the dining table or long buffet.

The épergne, with its collection of dessert dishes, tended to oust the single dessert serving dish that had been fashionable from the early years of the century. The so-called strawberry dish, usually circular **but sometimes oval**, and on occasion of fan-shape, is one of the most attractive examples of simple silver, its raised sides fluted into a dozen, sixteen or more panels, the rim also often scalloped to give even greater elegance. An en-

Charming chinoiserie style épergne with canopied stand topped by a pineapple, symbol of hospitality. By Thomas Pitts, who specialised in pierced work. 1762. Height 24 in. Private collection.

graved coat of arms, often merely a crest or cypher, usually adorned the plain centre, but in expensive and fine instances, there would be an engraved border in the Régence manner: strapwork and cartouches enclosing running foliage and masks, vases and so on, or perhaps the individual flutes would be enhanced with engraved hatching or other motifs. These were specialities of the grand silversmiths such as Lamerie. A few of the dishes were provided with cast scroll and foliage feet, but most were plain, and were made in all sizes, from little patty pans (for making pastry) about four inches across to larger versions about ten inches in diameter.

A few fine silver bowls of the period—other than sugar bowls—have survived. Some were quite plain, and perhaps used for broth or porridge, but others with fluted sides seem to have a kinship with the fluted dessert dishes of the period until about 1750. One fine bowl by George Wickes, dated 1744, stands on a chased foot, and has a deep spirally fluted body applied in alternate flutes with panels of shells and scrolls in the Rococo manner. A set of six deep bowls with engraved Rococo rims, but otherwise plain, were made by Edward Feline in 1749, while a set by S. Herbert & Co. made 1751 and 1752 have handled fluted bowls provided with stands of the strawberry-dish type—perhaps a mid 18th-century version of the out-of-date porringer for which the Huguenot-born silversmiths had no inclination and which died out with their establishment as leaders of style.

Silver plates and dishes continued to be made throughout the period and practical considerations obviously limited their style to plain moulded rims, gadrooning and, occasionally guilloche borders. Matching sets of dishes and plates were made over the years for wealthy patrons, often the work of several different silversmiths. The wear to which plates are subjected may have meant that of all English silver they suffered most in the melting-pot, but many splendid soup, main and second-course dishes have survived. About 1750 the **entrée dish** made its appearance, a shallow serving dish, square or cushion-shaped as a rule, but not provided with a cover. Indeed, only a few dish covers of the period seem to have survived at all.

39

One of seven dessert dishes, each on four scroll feet. Paul de Lamerie. 1734. Length 13½ in. The others are one large and four smaller circular dishes and another oval dish. Ashmolean Museum, Oxford.

Meat and fish dishes were made in a variety of patterns, such as the shaped oblong and the oval, some with fine-shaped shell and gadroon mounts and even with large shell motifs at either hand. Many were made in sets of various sizes. Accompanying

39 the fish dish was the **strainer or mazarin**, usually oval, but occasionally of circular form. The mazarin was simply a flat piece of plate with a narrow rim to fit over the well of the dish, pierced all over with scrolls and strapwork or other motifs. Four of the most beautiful mazarins ever made are dated 1762, two of them in the royal collection and two at Charlecote Park, each pierced and engraved with a net full of easily identifiable fish.

The twin problems of keeping food hot at table and keeping hot food from contact with the table both exercised the ingenuity of the silversmith. Dish-rings, established by 1700, were simple ring stands on which dishes or plates could be placed, but the need to keep foot hot as well was solved by adding a central brazier to the dish-ring. Small braziers or chafing dishes of this type were also made to fit saucepans of various sizes used at table.

41 About 1740 the less cumbersome **dish-cross** made its appearance, and continued in fashion until the end of the century. Shell or scroll feet were joined to the brackets which held the dish by means of a slot, through which the four arms of the cross were inserted. The arms were fixed to rings round the central lamp, so that they could both be swivelled to suit different sizes of dish or plate, and they could also be lengthened or shortened through the slots as required.

Knives, forks and spoons were perhaps the least ordered of

silver in the early Georgian period. Forks were still rarities, and made in much smaller numbers than spoons, while knives, with steel blades, have become damaged, rusted or lost over the years.

Soon after the accession of George II a new style of spoon, generally called the Hanoverian, began to replace the rat-tail. Instead of the rat-tail the stem terminated in a double drop, though the ridge along the front of the stem remained. Soon, however, that was shortened almost to extinction. The next variation had an almost identical bowl and a plain stem, but the end turned backwards instead of forwards slightly. This was the ubiquitous Old English pattern, which was in later years to be

right One of a set of four cushion shaped entrée dishes with gadrooned rims. Frederick Kandler. 1758. Width 9½ in. Private collection.

below Large mazarin or strainer dish, an early example pierced with scrolls, quatrefoils and dots in a geometrical arrangement. John Le Sage. 1742. Private collection.

showered with a variety of edge decoration, though not often prior to 1770.

Decoration on early Georgian spoons was chiefly confined to the teaspoon and the dessert service, with the exception of small numbers of table-spoons and serving spoons with fancy backs. The shell was the earliest detail to be used, from about 1740 onwards, but soon other ornaments were conceived, chiefly based on the Rococo shell and scroll, or foliage curving along the back of the bowl. From the end of the 1740s a pattern with a volute scroll terminal, called Onslow after the Speaker of the House of Commons, came into use. It was not made into table services, but ·was confined chiefly to servingspoons, soup ladles, sifter and caddy spoons and teaspoons. As early as the 1740s a few spoons are recorded with an incipient fiddle motif near the bowl, showing French influence, but they were not made in any quantity during the period.

Table forks, chiefly rather large, followed the various spoon patterns – rat-tail, Hanoverian and Old English, usually with three tines or prongs, though two-pronged steel forks with silver handles were frequently made, either with plain handles or with pistol-grip handles, usually stamped out, matching those of the scimitar-bladed knives.

Supplementing the flatware and cutlery were marrowscoops, pie- and fish-slices, basting spoons, ladles and skewers. Marrowscoops were made throughout the period in the standard form of a long scoop at one end with a narrower smaller scoop of a single piece of silver at the other. The only occasional concession to decoration was a shell on the back of the larger bowl, and engraved crest or other small piece of ornament. Very large scoops for the marrow of beef and other large bones were sometimes made on the end of basting spoons, which otherwise followed the style of tablespoons.

Pie- and fish-slices allowed the silversmith an opportunity to pierce out the blades in a variety of designs, and during the Rococo era a number of very charming slices were made. **A large**
41 **oval fish-slice** by Paul de Lamerie, made in 1741 and now in the Ashmolean Museum, has fish pierced and engraved amid the

scrolls and wave ornaments, while from the 1760s come slices pierced with foliage, birds and other Rococo motifs. Rococo shell themes were also popular on soup ladles, the bowl usually being formed as a shell, with the handle either of Hanoverian, Old English or Onslow pattern. Another silver requisite at table was the skewer, larger for meat, small and very slender for game. Plainness was practical, but shell and ring handles did bow to the Rococo, and one very rare, perhaps unique, set of 1749 have tapered foliate finials.

Superbly pierced fish-slice. Paul de Lamerie. 1741. Length $12\frac{1}{2}$ in. Ashmolean Museum, Oxford.

Dish stand or cross, on four shell feet with arms extending to $12\frac{1}{4}$ in. Most dish-crosses had central lamps for keeping the dish above warm. John Innes. 1751. Private collection.

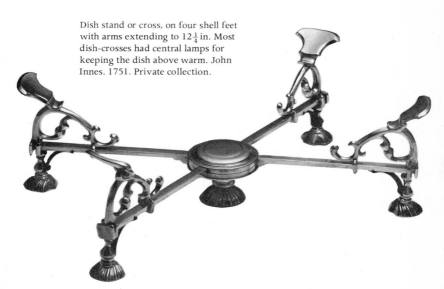

Chocolate and Coffee Pots and Tea-table Silver

Even more than the arrival of new silver for the dining-table, the drinking of tea, coffee and chocolate affected English silver during the first half of the 18th century. Hundreds of coffee pots, a myriad of accoutrements for the tea-table from pots and kettles to cream jugs, sugar tongs, and specially designed pots for chocolate were made in a wide variety of designs that reflected every change in taste over the period.

43   The basic form of the coffee pot was a **tall tapering cylinder**, usually fairly capacious, about $8\frac{1}{2}$ inches high. A moulded foot provided a firm base, and the handle, as a rule of wood or ivory, was held in plain silver sockets and was of scroll form. It was generally placed opposite the spout, occasionally at right-angles to it. Spouts were usually slightly curved and often faceted, and gradually more and more decorative motifs came to be applied to the bases of them. They might be scalloped, or chased with scrolls, and sometimes the top was capped with a leaf motif. A few pots have a moulded rib about halfway up the spout, the faceted surface below being filled with flat-chased or engraved decoration, but even after 1735 most pots were left plain except for ornament on the spout or handle sockets. The most usual concession to ornament was the elaboration of the cartouche containing the owner's arms. Even the finial on the low flat domed cover was usually still a plain urn, acorn or baluster shape.

     About 1735 some attempt was made to introduce new styles.
45   Some makers used French designs, with **pear-shaped bodies**

fluted overall and set on three cast feet or on a circular fluted and spreading foot. But soon coffee pot design settled for a practical slightly tapering body with a tuck-in base and moulded foot.

Chasing in low relief round the base and neck rim replaced the flat-chased borders of the first Rococo pots, and some magnificent asymmetrical Rococo ornament appeared on a number of coffee pots by makers such as Lamerie, Eliza Godfrey and Pezé Pilleau during the early 1740s. Most coffee pots, while following the new style and almost always making a decorative feature of the spout, remained otherwise plain. Some acquired chasing in later years, especially during the early 19th century and in the Victorian period—a headache to the novice who often finds it difficult to differentiate between contemporary Rococo chasing and later imitations.

left Tapering cylindrical coffee pot with flat-chased Rococo designs on body and octagonal spout. David Willaume. 1735. Height $7\frac{3}{4}$ in. Private collection.

right A more pronounced tuck-in base for a coffee pot with the owner's arms in an elaborate cartouche. Thomas Whipham and William Williams. 1741. Private collection.

By the late 1750s, a more pronounced **elongated baluster**
45 **shape** came into fashion, the appearance of height further accentuated by the double domed cover and tall flame or urn finial.
The formerly almost flat foot was now stepped and raised to a
sort of collar, and foot and rim mounts were frequently gadrooned while curved spout and scrolling handle sockets relieved
the otherwise plain sides. A few pots were chased with flower
festoons, chinoiseries and sometimes Rococo shellwork, but most
were plain and, as with mugs, tankards and cream jugs, decoration should be carefully examined to make sure that it is truly
contemporary.

Chocolate never attained anything like the popularity that it
had in France, and few pots specifically for chocolate were made.
Those that were had short lips, and were otherwise in the form
of covered baluster jugs.

Tea continued to be expensive, and pots relatively small; about
four and a half inches was the usual height. Until about 1740, the
45 teapot was of **globular or bullet-shape**, with a slightly tapered
straight spout, moulded foot, and cover in line with the body.
The style with the base slightly smaller than the shoulder was
highly suited to narrow bands of engraved or flat-chased ornament at the shoulders, concealing the joint with the cover.
Handles were mostly of wood, plain except for a slightly up-
turned thumb-piece, and a button-type finial of the same material
was usually on the cover, held by a silver fly screw. After about
1740, spouts tended to be curved, and were given ornamental
treatment with scrolls, scalloped edges and so on in the manner
of the coffee pots.

The next change was the fluted version of the bullet-shape,
with spreading fluted foot and curved fluted spout, and by about
1750 the round shape gave way to the inverted pear-shape, the
broad shoulders sometimes richly chased with Rococo shells,
scrollwork, flowers and foliage. A few rarities imitated ceramic
forms—occasionally a pot made in a typical Staffordshire pottery
shape is encountered, but basically the bullet-shape and the inverted pear-shape held sway until superseded by the oviform and
drum-shapes of the 1770s.

above Pear-shaped coffee pot chased in relief with Rococo scrolls, flowers and wave ornament. Eliza Godfrey. 1741. Height $9\frac{1}{2}$ in. Private collection.

below Typical bullet-shaped teapot on moulded circular foot, with tapered faceted spout and flat cover. John Le Sage. 1737. Height $4\frac{1}{2}$ in. Private collection.

above Coffee pot in the elongated pear-shape of the later period, chased with scrolls, flowers and a Chinese building below the Rococo cartouche. William Tuite. 1762. Victoria and Albert Museum, London.

Refilling the teapot was done at table from the **silver tea-kettle** kept boiling over its own lamp held in a stand. A globular shape conforming to the outline of the bullet teapot, with shoulders and flat lid ornamented with engraved or flat-chased arabesques and strapwork, typified those of the 1730s. Tea-kettles, however, always retained the curved spout, plain, faceted or with leaf-cap or scroll decoration, and featured a sturdy swing handle with insulating turned wooden section set on scroll supports.

The kettle stand with a circular spirit lamp supported in the centre was usually of tripod form—on rare occasions a free-standing piece of silver furniture some twenty-six or twenty-eight inches high. By 1730 it usually had shell feet, and the circular section below the actual rim for the kettle was pierced out as an apron above the spirit lamp. This was gradually made deeper to conceal the lamp, becoming more and more elaborately pierced and chased.

The fluted melon-shape that followed had a flat cover still in line with the body, but soon domed covers enriched with chasing were introduced, and the globular bodies were overlaid with festoons and repoussé chased with scrolls, shells and even with cupids or other figures in semi-relief. Others might show the Rococo themes with flat-chased scrolls, shells, diaperwork and flowers and foliage, either covering the whole body or, more often, the shoulders only, most of the decoration being lavished on the stand and apron and the spout of the kettle.

The kettle of the 1740s was also frequently of the inverted pear-shape, especially the more richly decorated examples by silversmiths such as Aymé Videau, Paul de Lamerie, Pezé Pilleau, Eliza Godfrey and Thomas Whipham. Yet even at the height of the period, a tea-kettle might be a riot of Rococo fantasy—in one example chased with marine motifs, in another with chinoiseries—or a simple spherical version with scarcely any concession to ornament, as instanced by three different kettles by Paul de Lamerie, all made in 1745.

Flower chasing and chinoiseries dominated the decorated kettles of the next twenty years, and most kettles retained the inverted pear-shape right up to the Adam period, though here

Large tea-kettle of the inverted pear-shape that dominated teapot and kettle styles between about 1745 and 1760. Chased with Rococo scrolls and flowers, the cast and pierced apron on the lampstand is also chased with masks, matching those on the tripod legs. Thomas Whipham. 1746. Private collection.

and there the old plain pear-shape might be revived, as in Thomas Heming's silver-gilt kettle, stand and lamp for Queen Charlotte, which has scrollwork around the shoulders echoed in the chased scrolls on the stand. From about 1725 onwards by far the most popular insulating covering for the handle was wicker, though leather was sometimes used, and occasionally ivory.

A newcomer to the tea-table was the tea-urn, of considerably larger capacity than the kettle. One of the earliest recorded is an oblong urn of 1746, with a tap on either end. Another early example was a Rococo extravaganza of 1752 by James Shruder, standing twenty-two inches high and weighing a grand total of 274 ounces. Dolphin feet to the stand are matched by three dolphin taps, while the pear-shaped body is chased with ships, dolphins and foliage on a matted ground, and the swing handle rises to a scroll from supports chased with bulrushes.

It was not, however, until the 1760s that tea-urns began gradually to replace kettles at the tea-table; they were vase-shaped or oviform, their shape heralding the new classicism to come, although sometimes chased with spiral fluting in the continental manner.

While teapots and tea-kettles tended to develop in a similar way, the making of matched tea services was the exception rather than the rule; few are recorded until the end of the period, and of those, all but one or two are composite services rather than matched sets of one date by one maker.

It is possible that a good many of the small waiters that survive were originally associated with coffee pots, teapots or kettles—the latter sometimes found with triangular waiters to suit the tripod lampstands.

Teaspoons were made in many designs. The plain Hanoverian pattern soon gave way to shell-backs, which appeared in great variety, and from about 1740 onwards these were further developed. Many fancy patterns were used on the backs of the bowls: roses, herons, the bird in a cage with 'I Love Liberty' made popular by the Wilkes fracas of 1762, ships, teapots and Prince of Wales's feathers as well as shells, scrolls and foliage motifs. Others were decorated on back and front of the stem with Rococo shells, grotesque masks, cherubs, Apollo and other motifs from about 1750 onwards, while a few really exotic tea-spoons, often gilt, were in the form of intertwined twigs, even crawling with tiny caterpillars, and the bowls formed as leaves.

Sugar tongs were of the scissor type, mostly quite plain, with scroll arms and loop handles, the grips of plain or shell form. Some of the more elaborate Rococo sets of nippers and teaspoons, sometimes found in association with tea-caddies, were gilt. About 1755, the springy U-type sugar tong was gradually introduced, the Rococo being interpreted by elaborately pierced arms and shell grips, the arms sometimes being twisted or set sideways on to display the ornament better.

Another small tea-table accessory was the strainer spoon, a spoon with an olive-shaped bowl pierced out with scrolls or crosses and usually with a tapering stem with diamond-shaped point at the end. A few had shell backs like the teaspoons of the period. They were used to remove leaves floating in the tea, and it is said that the long points were used to clear clogged leaves from the teapot spout.

Making the tea at table required at least one caddy, perhaps

49

two, in which the precious and expensive tea could be safely
locked away. The connoisseur needed two caddies, so that the
tea could be blended as required, and sometimes 'B' and 'G',
for black and green, are found engraved on the sides or base to
remind the hostess. A third box might also be made en suite for
sugar, the shape of the box usually being a little broader or
squatter than that of the tea caddies.

The engraved or flat-chased rectangular tea-caddy was trans-
formed by the Rococoists into an **elegant box** with the base and
shoulders chased in high relief with rocaille motifs, the covers
sliding and having hinged finials that lay flat in the often very
elaborate locked chests of shagreen, tortoiseshell, mother-of-
pearl or inlaid wood or ivory in which they were contained. A
few were provided with four cast feet, but most were flat based.

Tea-caddies were frequently more elaborately decorated than
other silver, and chinoiserie motifs were a natural and appropriate theme, though they were often mixed with Rococo ones,
such as European ladies under Chinese umbrellas amid high
Rococo shell and scrollwork. Shapes included the baluster vase,
often much chased with flowers and foliage, the plain oval and,
from about 1750, **the bombé**, a form derived from furniture.
Swirl-fluting was sometimes used for simpler versions of the
baluster caddy, sometimes interspersed with chased flowers and
foliage, or even with masks, figures, chinoiseries and anything

50

51

53

49

else, Rococo or Chinese, that would please the elegant hostess at the tea-table.

About 1760, for those tired of the much chased baluster and bombé forms, the tea-chest style caddy provided a novelty: a cube with a flat cover. The more restrained examples were engraved rather than chased, and there was a vogue for plain cubic or cylindrical caddies engraved with vertical panels simulating wooden tea-chests, and with Chinese characters on the slatting, although usually the borders were less oriental, having perhaps laurel foliage or even a Greek key pattern.

About 1730 to 1735, small fluted bowls without covers appeared, which were almost certainly used as sugar bowls.

left Unusual sugar bowl and cover in the form of a shell, symbol of the Rococo era. Christian Hilland. 1739. Private collection.

below Set of two siver-gilt caddies and sugar box combining Rococo scrolls, bats-wings, masks and teaplant finials with repoussé chased rustic huts, palm trees and Chinese harvesters. Paul de Lamerie. Caddies 1747. Sugar box 1750. Private collection.

The bombé shape on scroll bases for a set of caddies decorated with rocaille and diaper motifs and armorials in foliate Rococo cartouches. Fuller White. 1755. Private collection.

50 One rare and unusual sugar bowl of 1739, by Christian Hilland (a maker noted for his tea-caddies) is **formed as a shell**, the body and cover fluted all over. During the 1740s, the vase form was somewhat awkwardly adapted for the sugar, but by then the sugar for the tea-table was generally contained in a bowl or box made to go with the tea-caddies, and the receptacle lost its individual identity.

53 As the sugar bowl tended to become part of the caddy set, so the **cream jug** developed in its own way. In the 1730s Paul de Lamerie often favoured the helmet-shaped jug on a moulded foot, the stem formed as some grotesque creature such as a serpent or dragon. Three cast scroll feet were used on sturdy pear-shaped jugs with scroll handles and spreading lips, and about 1740 there was a tendency to produce lower jugs with bellied bodies, which must have been rather easier to clean than the narrow-necked pitcher styles.

Indeed, the cream boat on a central foot or on three cast feet gradually became more and more popular during the 1740s and 1750s, and many were cast and chased in the high Rococo manner. The taller jug styles persisted, however, often fluted or swirl-fluted and chased with typical Rococo flowers and foliage, though, as with the baluster coffee pots of the 1750s and 1760s, there was a fashion for decorating them later. Thus careful inspection of the style of decoration is advisable—a clue to the type of flower motifs used can be found in contemporary pottery jugs painted or embossed with flowers and foliage.

One curious form of cream jug made only between about 1753 and 1772 is the cow creamer. These **little jugs in the form of cows**, often realistically tooled, were almost all the work of one silversmith in London, John Schuppe, between 1755 and 1768. The earliest now creamer, perhaps the inspiration for Schuppe's work, is a rather plain version of 1753 by David Willaume (now in the Victoria and Albert Museum) and after his time, one by Edward Aldridge, made in 1769, is also very plain. The short period during which they were made naturally makes these little jugs rare, and they must always have been somewhat unhygienic, for the opening on the back with its fly finial is always small and the cow's mouth through which the cream was poured is also difficult to get at. They were, however, a pretty toy for the lady of the house who, even in London, and certainly during her summer sojourn in the country, must have had at least some knowledge of the dairy.

above Unusual nine-sided cream jug on three scroll and hoof feet. Edith Fletcher. 1729. Private collection.

left Sugar vase of classical form yet with Rococo fluting and shell motifs. Emick Romer. 1766. Private collection.

far left Cow creamer. John Schuppe. 1765. Schuppe specialised in making these creamers between about 1755 and 1768. Very few by other makers are known. Private collection.

Silver for Beer, Wine and Spirits

The sale of beer and ale in the 18th century suffered not only from the widespread use of tea and coffee, but from increased consumption of wines and spirits among all classes of society. The tankard, perhaps the least subject to changing styles of all English silverwares, was still made, but in relatively small quantities, especially in London. By about 1730, the shaped baluster form was firmly established, the scroll handle usually capped with a leaf motif to take the brunt of the knock as the lid swung back, while the thumbpiece was now almost standardised to an openwork scroll.

55   More common than tankards were the **small mugs**, probably mostly intended for use in the nursery and schoolroom, where, as the water supply was generally most unhygienic, small beer would still be the prevailing beverage. There was a little more attention to current fashions in these, with a pronounced baluster form becoming usual by the mid 1730s, though generally speaking any decoration other than engraved armorials or initials was rare and can usually be ascribed to a later date.

For wine and spirits, the expansion of the glassmaking trade meant diminution of demand for silver drinking vessels, but a

55   few beakers, wine cups and **tumbler cups** continued to be made. Tumbler cups, with their heavy bases that prevent them from tumbling over, were mostly made in pairs, presumably so that two could drink together. They were probably mostly used for spirits, and some are engraved with presentation inscriptions.

They vary in size, from about one and a half inches high to quite capacious cups as much as three inches high. Perhaps the rarest and finest pair of tumbler cups are associated with a larger pair of beakers. Made by Aymé Videau in 1743, the smaller pair are not strictly tumblers, as they have flattened bases, but all four are delightfully and finely engraved with different scenes, a 'love's progress' of the squire and the milkmaid, within elegant cartouches in the French manner.

The beaker remained a small, tapering cylinder on a narrow foot or assumed a bell-shape with everted lip until the 1760s, when paired drinking cups were sometimes fitted together to form a barrel. One such pair by Edward Aldridge, 1765, are actually engraved 'Hob' and 'Nob' to suggest drinking companions, and the beaker-barrel was a favourite form in the north, especially in Chester and in Scotland. But for the most part the beaker and the tumbler cup were confined to the traveller, forming part of the necessary canteen carried wherever soldier or tourist journeyed.

Baluster mug engraved with contemporary armorials. Gurney & Cook. 1738. Height 4¼ in. Private collection.

Tumbler cup of large size. Thomas Whipham & C. Wright. 1767. Height 2½ in. Collection Mrs. W. B. Munro, Pasadena, California.

Silver goblets came into fashion again about 1765, after a lapse of almost a century. Tulip-shaped bowls, a knopped stem and plain circular foot with a band of gadrooning were forerunners of the classical styles introduced by Adam, but in general wine glasses and rummers had swept the silver drinking vessel from the fashionable cupboard.

Serving wine was, however, a different matter, and the richest
57 households provided themselves with silver **wine fountains**, wine coolers, cisterns and jugs (the last also being used by those families where beer and ale were still drunk). Since such silverwares were necessarily large and expensive, they usually showed the latest taste and were made by the foremost silversmiths of the day. Keeping large quantities of wine cool in silver cisterns was an extravagant though magnificent way of displaying wealth. One of the largest and grandest of all must be that weighing 8,000 ounces (now in Russia) which was made by Charles Kandler in 1734 to a design of George Vertue, and was offered as a prize in 1735 in the lottery organised to raise money to build Westminster Bridge. In design it looks back to Renaissance magnificence, with curvaceous caryatid handles, its sides very richly chased with bacchantes, and supports for the base formed by four chained leopards. There is an electrotype copy in the Victoria and Albert Museum. From the end of the period comes another famous cistern–that of 1770 made by Thomas Heming in the latest French-inspired style. The shallow shaped body is chased with vines and scrolls, while the handles are formed as the royal supporters, for this was the Speaker's Plate of Sir John Cust, ancestor of Lord Brownlow at whose seat, Belton, the cistern remains.

Another rarity of the period was the wine cooler for a single bottle. One pair of 1727 by Thomas Farrer is vase-shaped, the lower parts of the bodies applied with strapwork–a forerunner of the grand wine coolers of the early 1800s. Equally rare was the wine fountain, in principle very like an urn, but about 1740 ducal and princely patrons seem to have ceased to use them or to have been content with those dating from earlier in the century.

About this time, silver bottle tickets, or wine labels as we now generally call them, came into use. Most early examples are shaped flattish pieces of silver, classified as escutcheons, and engraved or pierced with the name of the wine – burgundy, claret, sherry, madeira and champagne being among the most usual. A few wine tasters of the period exist, dating from the mid 18th century, plain and with the traditional domed centre, but in nothing like the numbers that have survived in France.

Among the most aesthetically satisfying of all early Georgian silverwares must be accounted the **jugs used for wine and beer**, some with covers, others unlidded. Apart from a very occasional inscription, there is nothing to differentiate between wine and beer jugs, though most unlidded jugs are usually called beer jugs, while covered jugs are sometimes called wine jugs.

57, 58

left Massive wine fountain by Peter Archambo. 1728. The piece is a 'duty dodger' – that is, the silversmith avoided paying the 6d. an ounce duty and inserted a small disc bearing hallmarks instead of sending it to the Assay Office. The Worshipful Company of Goldsmiths, London.

below Large plain baluster jug with unusual shell drop below the lip. William Shaw and William Priest. 1758. Private collection.

The baluster shape generally prevailed, with a circular foot and a bold scroll handle so that the jugs stood steady and handled easily when full. If a lid were provided, it was usually in the low domed style, with an urn or vase finial. Handles were usually of silver, since there was no problem of insulation. Such jugs were only occasionally much enriched with applied strapwork or chasing, the usual concession to ornament even during the Rococo period being perhaps a shell below the lip and a leaf cap to the handle. Towards the 1760s there was a tendency to elongate the rather squat baluster shape of the jug, and sometimes this new pear-shape was set on a high foot, the neck narrowed and then everted and shaped at the rim. Decorative jugs of this type were

Superb covered jug, one of a pair. Richly chased in relief with Rococo motifs, their use for beer is indicated by the pairs of putti with barrels surrounded by barley and hops. Phillips Garden. 1754. Height $13\frac{1}{2}$ in. Private collection.

sometimes chased with flower, scroll and foliate festoons, or very

58 appropriately, **with hops and barley or vine-leaf designs**. By the end of the 1760s, the bombé shape that developed out of the baluster was also used for jugs, but apart from chased detail around and below the short spout and at the top of the scroll handle, the traditional baluster style remained little changed until the advent of Neo-classicism, when the stable and sturdy jug of early Georgian England bowed to the tall vase-shaped Adam ewer.

For the well-to-do household, possession of a silver **punch**

66 **bowl** was a desirable social asset. These hemispherical bowls, mounted on a plain circular foot, were generally quite plain, unrelieved except for a finely engraved coat of arms in an elaborate cartouche. A few exceptions have fixed or detachable rims, a rather outdated style by the 1730s. It is interesting to note that a punch bowl was one of the pieces of plate run for at Westchester (Chester) Races, and by 1762 the bombé form was already being introduced, a style in later years to be depicted on the racecards.

A necessary accompaniment to the punch bowl was the ladle. Plain ladles with deep hemispherical bowl and tapering handle of silver, wood or ivory soon gave way to a more fanciful Rococo style, with shell-chased motifs at the handle socket and fluted sides; one fine specimen of 1740 by Phillips Garden has the bowl in the form of a double shell, but more commonly the punch ladle of the period from about 1740 to 1760 was an oval, lipped at one end and in the finer versions fluted at the edges. On good ladles, attention was paid to the joint between the bowl and the handle socket, but many were quite thin, almost mass-produced lines for the silversmith.

Also required for punch-making was a brandy warmer, and

67 here the **small saucepan** was much used, almost invariably of baluster shape, with a short lip and a turned wood side handle set at an upward angle. Most were quite small, perhaps two or three inches in diameter, and they were rarely decorated. Another piece of equipment at the punch table was a large strainer, sometimes supplied with a hook to hang on the edge of the bowl. These strainers, used for both lime and lemon, are usually pierced out

in simple geometrical patterns, but occasionally the ritual of brewing the punch was enriched by those with cast openwork handles instead of the more usual shaped 'ears', and one magnificent pair of strainers, made by William Plummer in 1767, have the bowls ribbed into panels pierced with scrolls and the handles elaborately cast in an openwork design of shells, grapes and scrolls. Measuring $11\frac{3}{4}$ inches overall, such strainers could easily be placed across the rim of a small punch bowl. Nutmeg graters, silver-mounted lime and lemon presses and a variety of strainer spoons completed the punch drinker's ritual equipment.

left Punch bowls, even at the height of the Rococo period, were usually plain, of slightly compressed form, as this one by David Willaume made in 1730. Diameter $10\frac{1}{4}$ in. Private collection.

left Baluster saucepan, unusual in having rocaille flat-chased ornament; most were quite plain. David Willaume. 1743. Formerly in the Ilchester collection.

Hallmarks 1727-1770

Apart from new regulations made in 1739 concerning the maker's mark, there were no major changes in hallmarking during the period.

THE ASSAY OFFICES. London, using the leopard's head crowned for sterling silver, remained the chief centre throughout the century. Three provincial offices were still functioning, all using the leopard's head crowned mark as well as their individual town marks. They were Chester (the three lions of England dimidiating the three garbs of the Earldom of Chester); Exeter (a triple-towered castle) and Newcastle (a castle arranged as two towers above a single tower). Officially there was still an office at York, but it did not appear to mark silver from about 1717 to 1773. Only one other provincial English office has been identified during the 18th century: Bristol, where a few pieces have been found bearing the mark of a ship issuing from a castle, used in association with the usual sterling marks.

THE STANDARD. Sterling silver was the normal standard, and was marked with the lion passant. After 1720, however, the higher Britannia standard (958 parts per 1000 pure silver instead of sterling's 925 parts) remained legal, and continued to be marked with the figure of Britannia and the lion's head erased. It is notable that the standard was used for some exceptional pieces, and that Paul de Lamerie did not use the sterling standard at all until 1732.

THE DATE LETTERS. London continued the usual twenty year cycle, omitting J, V, W, X, Y and Z. New series started in 1716 (capital

Roman letters) were followed by small letters starting in 1736 and blackletter capitals in 1756.

The Chester series covered twenty-five years (omitting J) with script capitals starting in 1726, and small letters in 1751.

Exeter omitted J and V, so that a twenty-four year cycle started in 1725 with small letters, in 1759 with capitals.

At Newcastle until 1758 a nineteen-year cycle was used, without J, or U–Z. In 1759 a new twenty-five year series, without J, began.

THE MAKER'S MARK. The usual form of mark consisted of the maker's or makers' initials of forename and surname, sometimes in association with a symbol such as a cup, star or crown. In an effort to prevent duty-dodging, in 1739 makers were obliged to register new marks. Many silversmiths had managed to avoid

Lion passant, leopard's head crowned for London, small u for 1755 and mark of Eliza Godfrey (the lozenge indicates her status as a widow) on sauceboats.

Very rare mark on Bristol-made beer jug of about 1740 shows the town arms, a ship issuing from a castle.